First Shapes

Premières Formes

Primeras Formas

Erste Formen

Prime Forme

Ivan and Jane Clark Chermayeff

Harry N. Abrams, Inc.,

Publishers, New York

Shapes are used to describe and to remember. Shapes can be added onto or carved out of. They can be arranged in patterns: up, down, and every way. Simple shapes are best, but the compli-cated ones can be nice, too.

A *square* has four sharp corners. It has two sides and a top and a bottom that are the same size. Turn it on a corner and it becomes a *diamond.* Push or pull two sides of a square and it is a *rectangle.* A *triangle* will always have three sharp corners instead of four.

A *circle* has one big side that goes all the way around. A circle is often found in the center of things... for instance, where a pebble has been dropped in a pool of water.

If a tiny circle has no hole, then it is a *dot.* When it is flattened out a little, as though some-one sat on it, it becomes an *oval.* If a circle inside another circle is very big and only leaves a little bit of the out-side circle on one side, it makes a *crescent.* Sometimes the moon is a crescent shape.

A *heart* has a dent in the round part on top of a

circle, which makes two puffed-out places. It is pointed on the opposite side, usually on the bottom... unless it is an upside-down heart. There are thin hearts and fat hearts, just as there are thin and fat girls and boys and dogs and cats.

Sometimes sides or lines that don't connect make shapes. Back-and-forth lines make a saw shape called a *zigzag*; but when the line just rolls along, it is called a *wave*, because it looks like the surface of a sea.

One up-and-down line, with another across the middle, makes a *cross*. If a line goes around and around and around, getting bigger and bigger, it is a *spiral*.

Petals and parts spinning and turning, *stars* and *pinwheels* are like flowers with five, six, twelve, or more points.

The world of shapes is the world around us. When you learn to recognize shapes, you are on your way to knowing a lot about a lot of things.

Looking and seeing provides endless opportunities for exploration and learning, and that is what this book is all about.

I.C. & J.C.C.

square le carré el cuadrado das Quadrat il quadrato

| diamond | le losange | el diamante | das Karo | il diamante |
| triangle | le triangle | el triángulo | das Dreieck | il triangolo |

circle

le cercle
el círculo
der Kreis
il cerchio

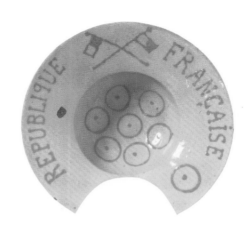

dot

le point
el punto
der Punkt
il punto

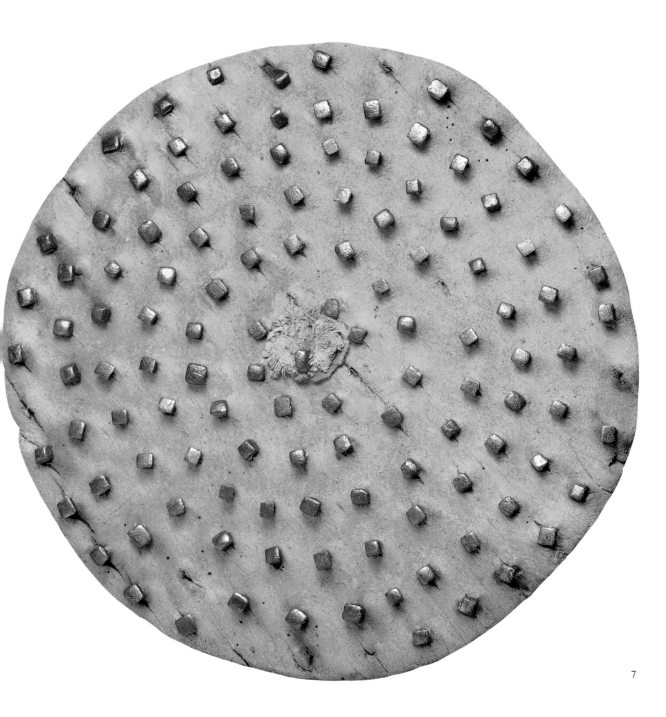

heart

le coeur
el corazón
das Herz
il cuore

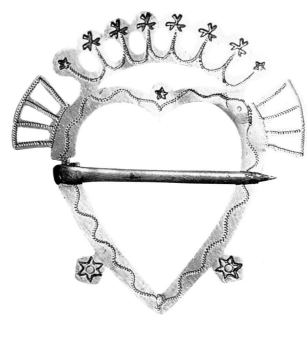

circle

le cercle
el círculo
der Kreis
il cerchio

zigzag

le zigzag
el zigzag
der Zickzack
lo zigzag

triangle

le triangle
el triángulo
das Dreieck
il triangolo

spiral

la spirale
la espiral
die Spirale
la spirale

oval

l'ovale
el óvalo
das Oval
l'ovale

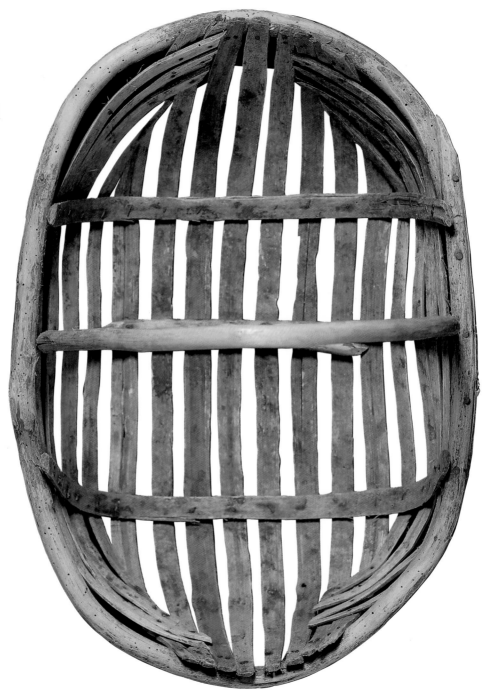

crescent

le croissant
la creciente
die Mondsichel
la mezzaluna

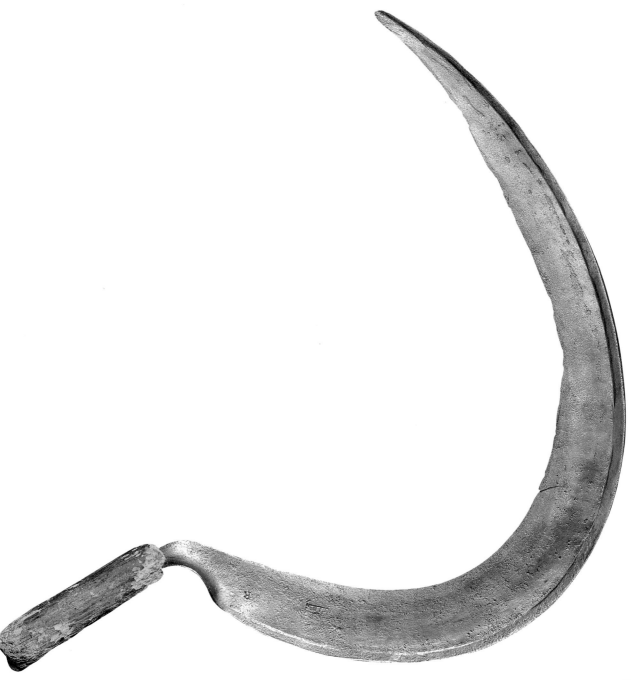

13

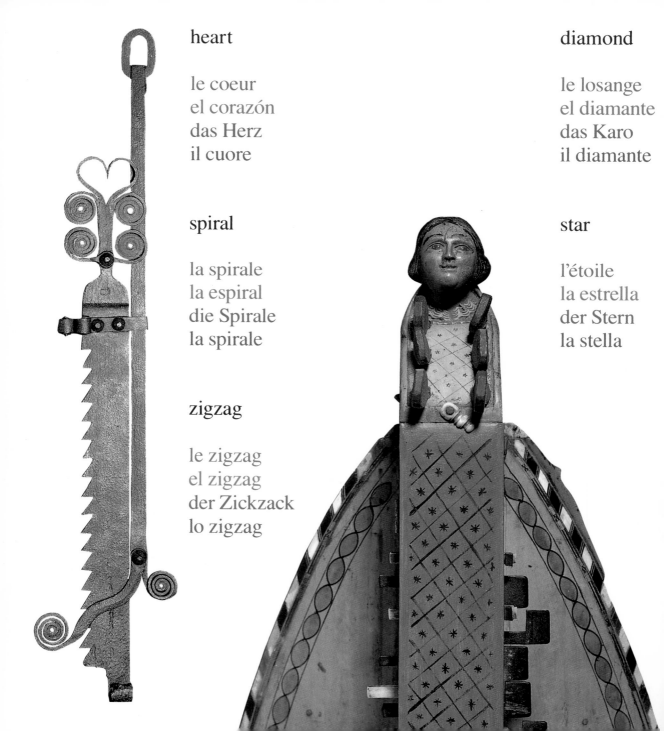

heart

le coeur
el corazón
das Herz
il cuore

spiral

la spirale
la espiral
die Spirale
la spirale

zigzag

le zigzag
el zigzag
der Zickzack
lo zigzag

diamond

le losange
el diamante
das Karo
il diamante

star

l'étoile
la estrella
der Stern
la stella

cross

la croix
la cruz
das Kreuz
la croce

clover

le trèfle
el trébol
das Kleeblatt
l trifoglio

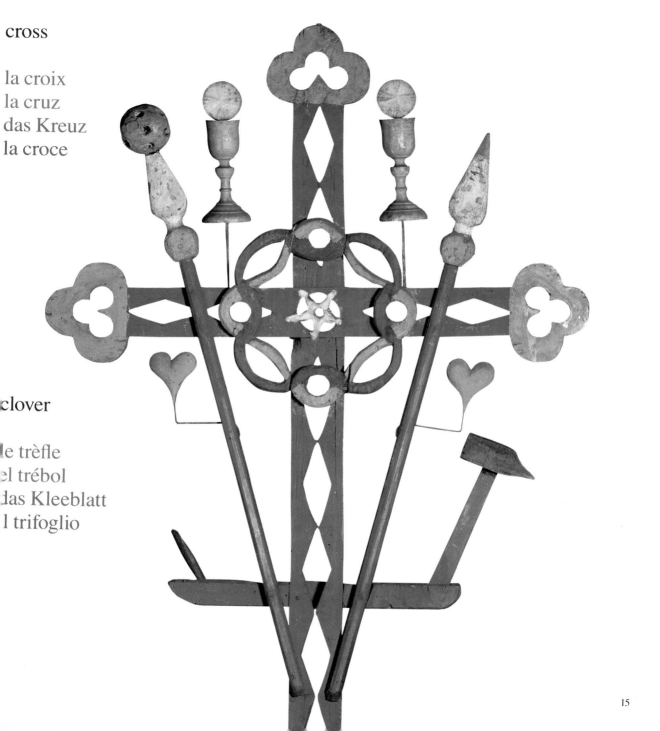

heart

le coeur
el corazón
das Herz
il cuore

circle

le cercle
el círculo
der Kreis
il cerchio

dot

le point
el punto
der Punkt
il punto

diamond

le losange
el diamante
das Karo
il diamante

square

le carré
el cuadrado
das Quadrat
il quadrato

rectangle

le rectangle
el rectángulo
das Rechteck
il rettangolo

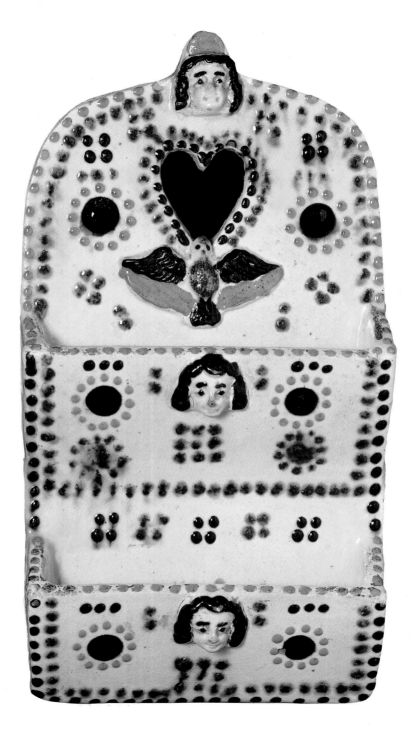

wave

la vague
la onda
die Welle
l'onda

zigzag

le zigzag
el zigzag
der Zickzack
lo zigzag

19

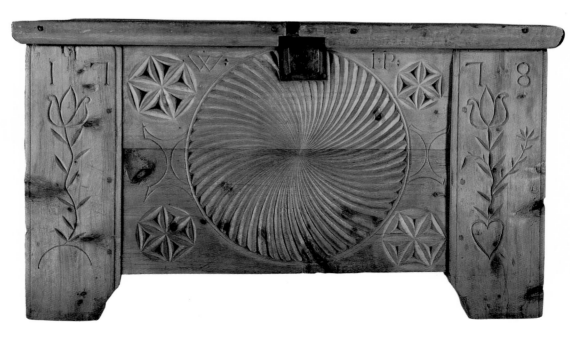

pinwheel   l'hélice   el molinete   das Windrädchen   la girandola

21

star

l'étoile
la estrella
der Stern
la stella

circle

le cercle
el círculo
der Kreis
il cerchio

23

cross

la croix
la cruz
das Kreuz
la croce

circle

le cercle
el círculo
der Kreis
il cerchio

diamond

le losange
el diamante
das Karo
il diamante

triangle

le triangle
el triángulo
das Dreieck
il triangolo

clover

le trèfle
el trébol
das Kleeblatt
il trifoglio

heart

le coeur
el corazón
das Herz
il cuore

arrow

la flèche
la flecha
der Pfeil
la freccia

fan	cross	star	pinwheel
l'éventail	la croix	l'étoile	l'hélice
el abanico	la cruz	la estrella	el molinete
der Fächer	das Kreuz	der Stern	das Windrädchen
l ventaglio	la croce	la stella	la girandola

tar pinwheel

étoile l'hélice
a estrella el molinete
er Stern das Windrädchen
a stella la girandola

ot square

e point le carré
l punto el cuadrado
er Punkt das Quadrat
punto il quadrato

square	le carré	el cuadrado	das Quadrat	il quadrato
	lə KA-ray	el KWAH-dra-doh	das KWAH-drat	il kwad-RA-toh
diamond	le losange	el diamante	das Karo	il diamante
	lə lə-ZĀ(N)ZH	el dee-ah-MAHN-tay	das KAH-roh	il dee-ya-MAHN-tay
rectangle	le rectangle	el rectángulo	das Rechteck	il rettangolo
	lə rehk-TĀ(N)GL	el rek-TAHN-goo-loh	das REHCHT-ehk	il ray-TAHN-goh-loh
triangle	le triangle	el triángulo	das Dreieck	il triangolo
	lə tree-Ā(N)GL	el tree-AHN-goo-loh	das DRY-ehk	il tree-AHN-goh-loh
oval	l'ovale	el óvalo	das Oval	l'ovale
	loh-VAL	el OH-vah-loh	das oh-VAHL	loh-VAH-lay
circle	le cercle	el círculo	der Kreis	il cerchio
	lə SEHRKL	el SEER-koo-loh	dehr KRICE	il CHAIR-kee-oh
dot	le point	el punto	der Punkt	il punto
	lə PWĀ(N)	el POON-toh	dehr POONKT	il POON-toh
heart	le coeur	el corazón	das Herz	il cuore
	lə KƏR	el ko-rah-SON	das HEHRTZ	il KWOH-ray
crescent	le croissant	la creciente	die Mondsichel	la mezzaluna
	lə krwa-SĀH(N)	la kray-see-EN-tay	dee MOHNT-zee-chəl	la metz-a-LOON-a
zigzag	le zigzag	el zigzag	der Zickzack	lo zigzag
	lə ZEEG-zag	el ZEEG-zahg	dehr TZIK-tzak	lo ZIG-zag
cross	la croix	la cruz	das Kreuz	la croce
	la KRWA	la KROOS	das KROYTZ	la KROH-chay
spiral	la spirale	la espiral	die Spirale	la spirale
	la spee-RAL	la es-PEE-rahl	dee spee-RAHL-ə	la spee-RA-lay
star	l'étoile	la estrella	der Stern	la stella
	lay-TWAL	la es-TRAY-yah	dehr SHTERN	la STEHL-lah
pinwheel	l'hélice	el molinete	das Windrädchen	la girandola
	LAY-leece	el moh-lee-NAY-tay	das VINT-rade-chen	la jee-RAHN-doh-la
clover	le trèfle	el trébol	das Kleeblatt	il trifoglio
	lə TREHFL	el TRAY-bol	das KLAY-blat	il tree-FOHL-lyoh
fan	l'éventail	el abanico	der Fächer	il ventaglio
	lay-vē(n)-TY	el ah-bah-NEE-koh	dehr FEHCH-er	il ven-TAHL-lyoh
arrow	la flèche	la flecha	der Pfeil	la freccia
	la FLEHSH	la FLAY-chah	dehr PFILE	la FREH-cha
wave	la vague	la onda	die Welle	l'onda
	la VAG	la OHN-da	dee VEHL-ə	LOHN-da

uare, diamond, triangle, pp. 4–5 *(clockwise from left):*

ay. 19th c. Woven straw. DH
aying cards: four and five of diamonds. 19th c. Paper,
4½ x 3″ (11.25 x 7.5 cm). SP
azier (early charcoal grill). 17th–18th c. Ceramic. DH

rcle, dot, pp. 6–7 *(counterclockwise from top left):*

rber's bowl commemorating the Republic. 1848. Ceramic,
″ (25 cm) diameter. SP
ule" ball. Wood with metal. DH
ule" ball. Wood with metal. DH
estnut cracker. 19th c. Wood with metal. DH

art, pp. 8–9 *(counterclockwise from top left):*

sket with lid. Woven straw. DH
inking horn. 19th c. Horn with wood, c. 13″ (32.5 cm) high. DH
staff (detail). 19th c. Wood with pewter. SP
ck. Iron. DH
sket for draining cheese. Early 20th c. Woven bark strips,
e″ (11.25 cm) wide. DH
ooch. 18th c. Silver, 1⅖″ (3.5 cm) high. SP

rcle, zigzag, triangle, spiral, oval, pp. 10–11 *(from left to right):*

staff (detail). First half 19th c. Wood with pewter. SP
old for fried dough. Iron. DH
sket. Woven wood strips. DH

Crescent, pp. 12–13 *(from left to right):*

Statue of Saint Isidore. 18th c. Painted wood. SP
Sickle. Steel and wood. DH

Heart, spiral, zigzag, diamond, star, cross, clover. pp. 14–15
(from left to right):

Fireplace kettle hook. 18th–19th c. Iron. DH
Stringed instrument (detail). Inlaid wood. DH
Processional cross (detail). Wood. DH

Heart, circle, dot, diamond, square, rectangle. pp. 16–17
(clockwise from left):

Comb holder. 2nd half 19th c. Ceramic. DH
Patterned wallpaper (detail). 19th–20th c. DH
Patterned wallpaper (detail). 19th–20th c. DH

Wave, zigzag, pp. 18–19 *(from left to right):*

Patterned wallpaper (detail). 19th–20th c. DH
Stringed instrument (detail). Inlaid wood. DH
Frame for winding lace. 19th c. Wood, 7 x 5¾″ (17.8 x 14.3 cm). SP

Pinwheel, pp. 20–21 *(counterclockwise from top left):*

Chest. 18th c. Wood, 44 x 22 x 27″ (110 x 55 x 67.5 cm). SP
Chest. 1778. Wood. SP
Box. Wood. DH
Quimper plate. 19th c. Ceramic. SP
Sarthe plate. 1889. Ceramic, 8″ (20.3 cm) diameter. SP

Star, circle, pp. 22–23 *(counterclockwise from top left):*

Cake mold. Ceramic. DH
Milk mug. Late 19th c. Wood. DH
Quarry hammerhead *(center)*. Iron. DH
Wafer iron. 18th c. Iron. DH
Box. Wood. DH

Cross, pp. 24–25 *(counterclockwise from top left):*

Pendant. 19th c. Silver. SP
Mariner's cross. Iron. DH
Ceremonial cross. Wood and straw. DH
Statue of Saint Éloi. Early 19th c. Painted wood. SP
Soup plate. First half 19th c. Ceramic. SP

Circle, diamond, triangle, clover, heart, arrow, fan, cross, star,
pinwheel, pp. 26–27 *(from left to right):*

Oil-lamp bracket. 18th–19th c. Wood. DH
Oil-lamp bracket. 18th–19th c. Wood. DH
Fireplace panel. 1840. Stone. SP

Star, dot, pinwheel, square, pp. 28–29 *(from left to right):*

Embroidered belt (detail). c. 1900. 62 x 392″ (155 x 940 cm). DH
Area rug. Early 20th c. Embroidered squares sewn together. SP

Editor: Harriet Whelchel
Designer: Ivan Chermayeff

Library of Congress Cataloging-in-Publication Data

Chermayeff, Ivan.
First shapes: premières formes, primeras formas, erste Formen,
prime forme / Ivan and Jane Clark Chermayeff.
p.   cm.

Summary: Works from France's Musée National des Arts et
Traditions Populaires introduce seventeen shapes and the many wa
they can be used and expressed by artists and craftsmen. Each shap
is listed in English, French, Spanish, German, and Italian.
ISBN 0–8109–3819–7

1. Design—Juvenile literature. 2. Visual perception—Juvenile
literature. [1. Shape. 2. Visual perception. 3. Art appreciation.
4. Polyglot materials.]
I. Chermayeff, Jane Clark, 1949–   .   II. Title.
NK1520.C47 1991   90–476
701′.8—dc20   C

Published in 1991 by Harry N. Abrams, Incorporated, New York
A Times Mirror Company

Printed and bound in Hong Kong